THE BOMBING OF PEARL HARBOR

written by
Joe Dunn

illustrated by
Joseph Wight with Rod Espinosa

red
wagon

visit us at
www.abdopublishing.com

Published by Red Wagon, a division of the ABDO Publishing Group, 8000 West 78th Street, Edina, Minnesota 55439. Copyright © 2008 by Abdo Consulting Group, Inc. International copyrights reserved in all countries. All rights reserved. No part of this book may be reproduced in any form without written permission from the publisher. Graphic Planet™ is a trademark and logo of Red Wagon.

Printed in the United States.

Written by Joe Dunn
Illustrated by Joseph Wight with Rod Espinosa
Colored and lettered by Joseph Wight
Edited by Stephanie Hedlund
Interior layout and design by Antarctic Press
Cover art by Rod Espinosa
Cover design by Neil Klinepier

Library of Congress Cataloging-in-Publication Data

Dunn, Joeming W.
    The Bombing of Pearl Harbor / Joe Dunn ; illustrated by Joseph Wight with Rod Espinosa.
    p. cm. -- (Graphic History)
    Includes bibliographical references and index.
    ISBN 978-1-60270-074-1
    1. Pearl Harbor (Hawaii) Attack on, 1941--comic books, strips, etc. 2. Graphic novels. I. Wight, Joseph. II. Espinosa, Rod. III. Title.

D767.92 .D85 2008
940.54'26693--dc22   2007004351

TABLE of CONTENTS

Chapter 1
The Signal...4

Chapter 2
The Launch..10

Chapter 3
The Attack Begins..16

Chapter 4
The *Arizona* Sinks..22

Chapter 5
War Is Declared...25

Timeline...30

Glossary...31

Web Sites...31

Index...32

Tuesday, December 2, 1941, Pacific Northern Sea.

The Imperial Japanese Aircraft Carrier *Akagi* emerges from a dark storm into a dense fog.

Aboard the *Akagi*, Vice Admiral Chuichi Nagumo, Commander of a vast Japanese fleet, peers through the fog from the bridge.

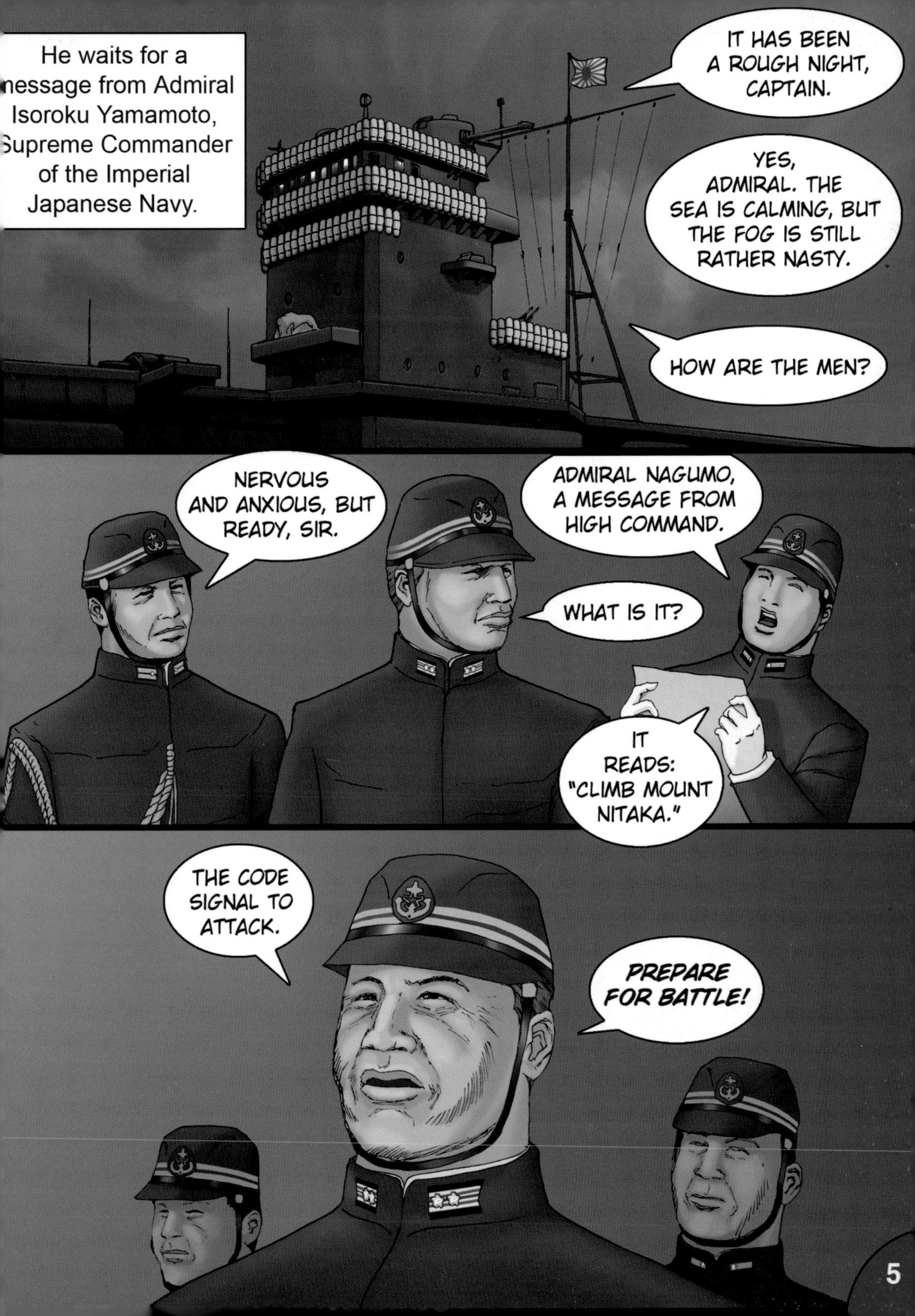
He waits for a message from Admiral Isoroku Yamamoto, Supreme Commander of the Imperial Japanese Navy.
IT HAS BEEN A ROUGH NIGHT, CAPTAIN.
YES, ADMIRAL. THE SEA IS CALMING, BUT THE FOG IS STILL RATHER NASTY.
HOW ARE THE MEN?
NERVOUS AND ANXIOUS, BUT READY, SIR.
ADMIRAL NAGUMO, A MESSAGE FROM HIGH COMMAND.
WHAT IS IT?
IT READS: "CLIMB MOUNT NITAKA."
THE CODE SIGNAL TO ATTACK.
PREPARE FOR BATTLE!

For 250 years, Japan had lived under the rule of the shoguns. They had isolated Japan from the rest of the world.

But in 1853, four U.S. Navy ships entered Tokyo Bay to set up trade relations.

The Japanese had never seen a steamship or even a cannon before. Japan began to see the rest of the world as a dangerous collection of nations. Shogun rule collapsed.

Japan installed an Emperor named "Meiji," which meant "Enlightened Ruler."

Japan rapidly became an aggressive, modern nation. It was determined to seize land and resources from surrounding countries.

The next 30 years would transform Japan into a nation of fanatics devoted to the Emperor and possessing a vast, well-equipped army and navy.

In 1937, Japan unleashed this mighty force on neighboring China.

In 1939, the United States ended trade relations, including the export of fuel and iron, with Japan. A large part of the American fleet moved to Pearl Harbor, Hawaii.

Japan responded by allying itself with Nazi Germany and Facist Italy, who were in the process of conquering Europe.

Two years later, a massive Japanese fleet of ships made its way to Hawaii to destroy the American Fleet anchored there.

It was meant to end American interference in Japan's conquest of the Pacific.

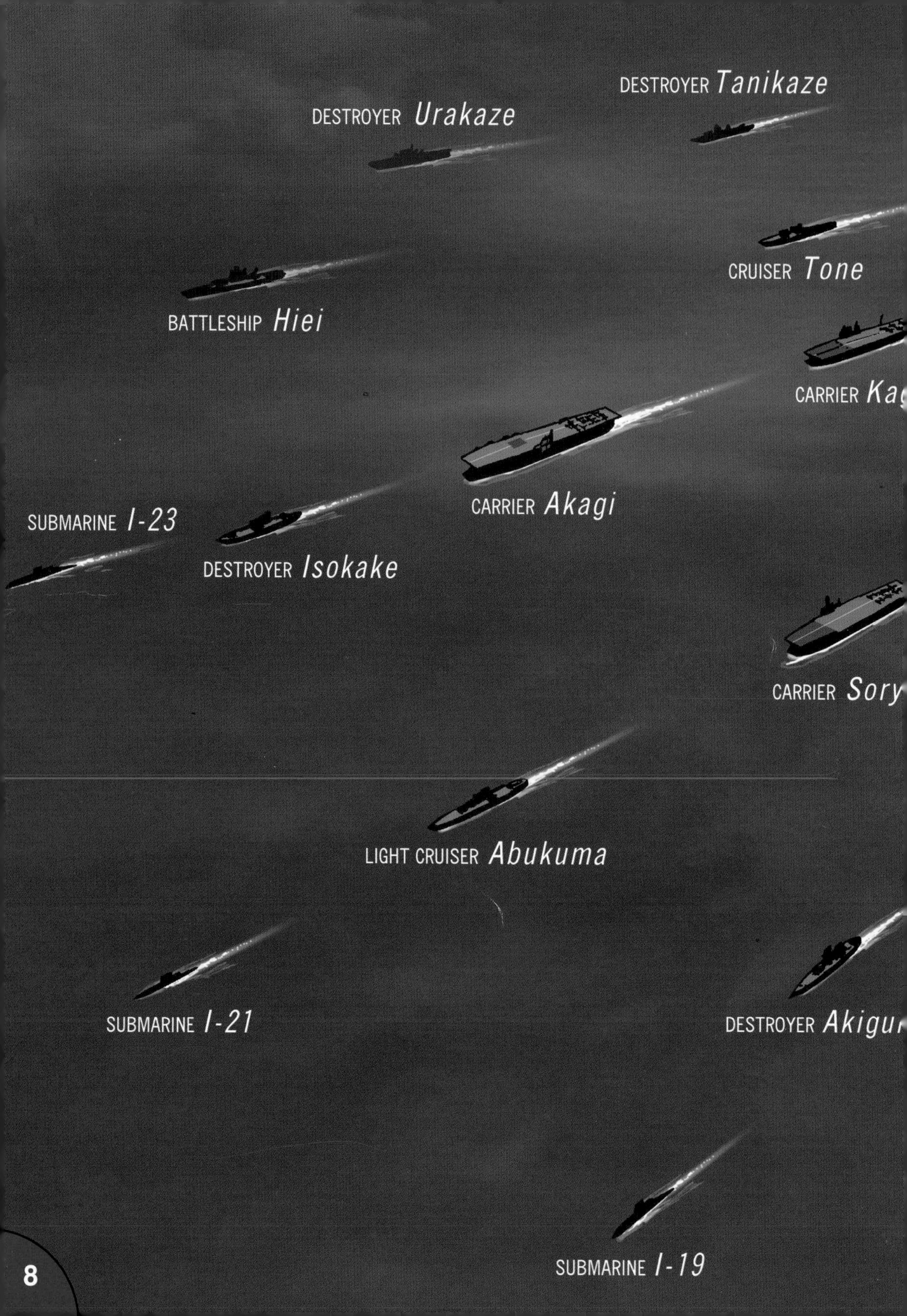
DESTROYER Tanikaze
DESTROYER Urakaze
CRUISER Tone
BATTLESHIP Hiei
CARRIER Ka
CARRIER Akagi
SUBMARINE I-23
DESTROYER Isokake
CARRIER Sory
LIGHT CRUISER Abukuma
SUBMARINE I-21
DESTROYER Akigu
SUBMARINE I-19

DESTROYER *Hamakaze*

DESTROYER *Arare*

DESTROYER *Kasumi*

CARRIER *Shokaku*

CARRIER *Zuikaku*

CRUISER *Chikuma*

TANKERS

CARRIER *Hiryu*

DESTROYER *Kagero*

DESTROYER *Shiranui*

BATTLESHIP *Kirishima*

The Japanese fleet consists of six aircraft carriers,
two battleships, two heavy cruisers, one light cruiser,
nine destroyers, three submarines, and six tankers.
The aircraft to be used were of three types:
79 "Zero" fighters, 143 "Kate" torpedo/horizontal
bombers, and 128 "Val" dive-bombers.

Chapter 2 The Launch

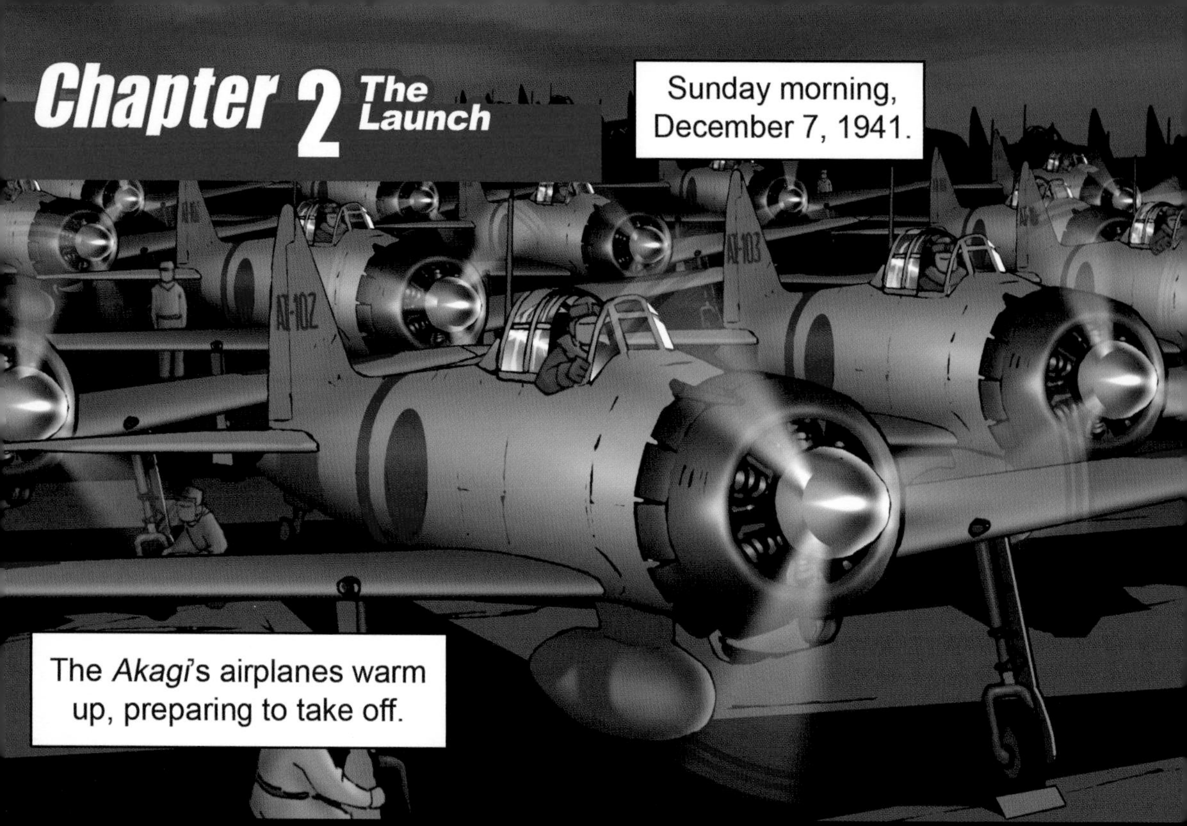
Sunday morning, December 7, 1941.
AI-102
AI-103
The *Akagi*'s airplanes warm up, preparing to take off.

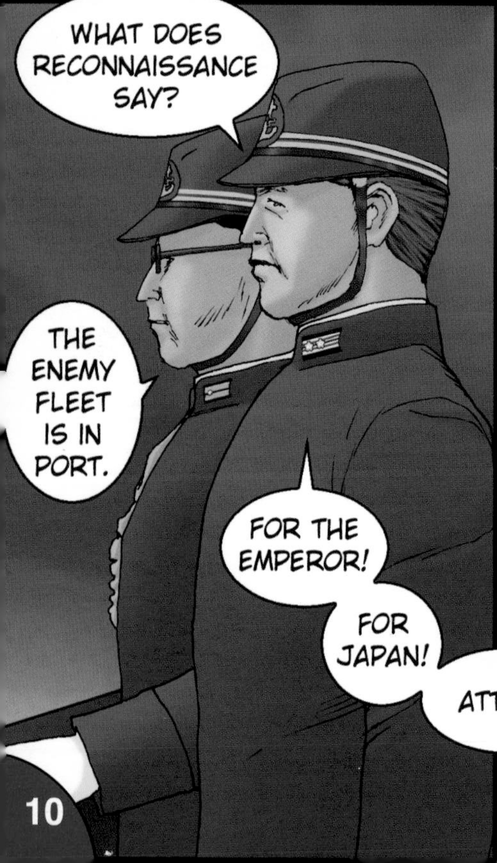
WHAT DOES RECONNAISSANCE SAY?
THE ENEMY FLEET IS IN PORT.
FOR THE EMPEROR!
FOR JAPAN!
ATTACK!

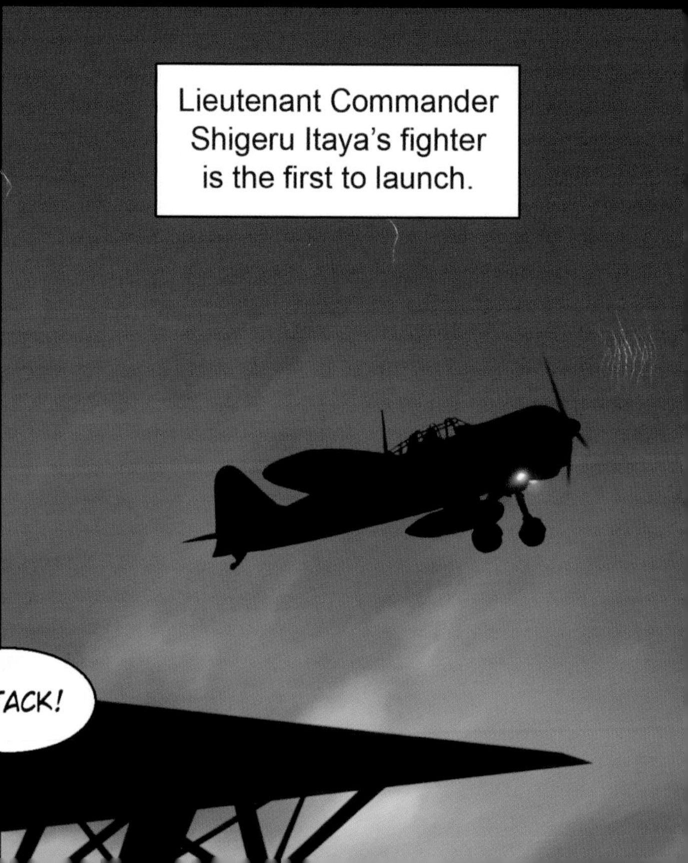
Lieutenant Commander Shigeru Itaya's fighter is the first to launch.

The planes launch six at a time. The first wave consists of 189 planes leaving from 6 carriers. It only takes 15 minutes for the first wave to become airborne.

The second attack wave has 167 planes.

The angry dragon is about to awaken the sleeping giant.

FIRST ATTACK WAVE

SECOND ATTACK WAVE

FIGHTERS

FIGHTERS

FIGHTERS

DIVE-BOMBERS

HORIZONTAL BOMBERS

Wheeler Field

TORPEDO BOMBERS

NAS Kaneohe

DIVE-BOMBERS

DIVE-BOMBERS

Ford Island

Pearl Harbor

Bellows Field

Hickam Field

HORIZONTAL BOMBERS

MCAS EWA

JAPANESE SUBMARINES

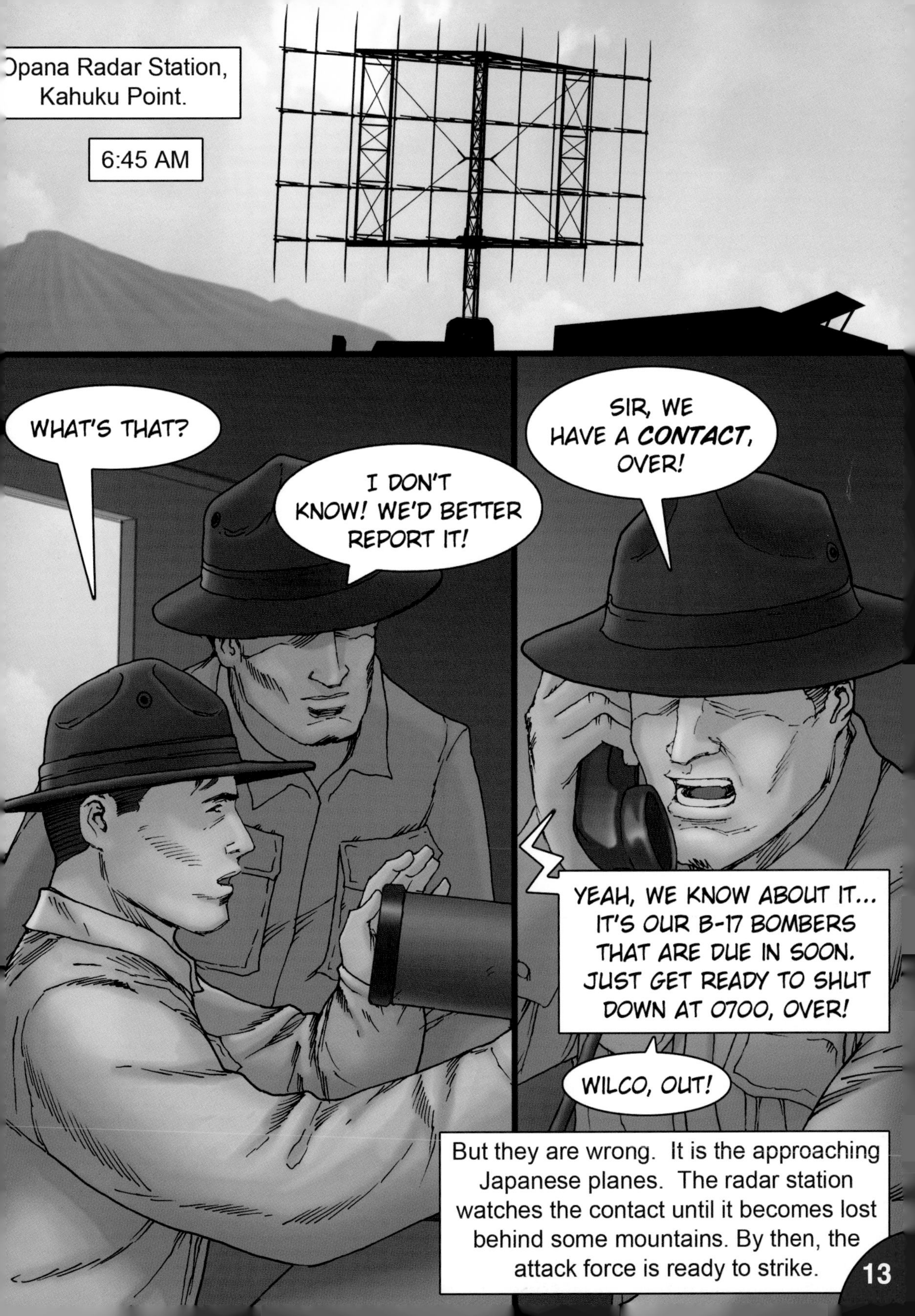
Opana Radar Station,
Kahuku Point.
6:45 AM
WHAT'S THAT?
I DON'T KNOW! WE'D BETTER REPORT IT!
SIR, WE HAVE A ***CONTACT***, OVER!
YEAH, WE KNOW ABOUT IT... IT'S OUR B-17 BOMBERS THAT ARE DUE IN SOON. JUST GET READY TO SHUT DOWN AT 0700, OVER!
WILCO, OUT!
But they are wrong. It is the approaching Japanese planes. The radar station watches the contact until it becomes lost behind some mountains. By then, the attack force is ready to strike.

At 7:40 AM, Flight Commander Mitsuo Fuchida fires a flare to signal his planes to commence the attack.

He follows up on his radio at 7:49 AM with the attack code: "TO...TO...TO..."

By 7:53 AM, with his planes poised to strike, Fuchida is confident that total surprise has been achieved.

He sends the famous radio signal "TORA, TORA, TORA" (TIGER, TIGER, TIGER– COMPLETE SURPRISE SUCCESSFUL) to the Japanese High Command before the first bomb is dropped.

It is a typical Sunday morning for American sailors and soldiers.

Some are preparing for the Colors Ceremony at 8:00 AM.

Others are having breakfast.

Families are leaving their homes for church.

Then, without warning...

At 7:55 AM, Japanese dive-bombers howl from the skies over Hickam and Wheeler Army Air Bases and Ford Island's Naval Air Station.

Their bombs destroy vulnerable planes and hangars. Fighters also join this attack, strafing the bases with their machine guns.

Two minutes later, Japanese torpedo planes skim across Pearl Harbor.

They deliver specially designed torpedos against Battleship Row.

These had been modified to perform in the shallow harbor waters.

The U.S. battleship *Oklahoma* is hit by at least 5 torpedos in the first 15 minutes of the strike.

The *Oklahoma* quickly begins to flood and roll to port (left). She will eventually turn upside-down, trapping 400 men in her hull.

Only 32 are rescued.

The battleships *California*, *West Virginia*, *Nevada* and *Utah* are also hit by torpedos in the rapid attack.

17

The Americans, realizing they are under massive attack, begin firing into the skies at the swarming Japanese planes.

American pilots rush to get to their planes, but are strafed by fighters before they can get airborne.

The American fighters and bombers, lined up tightly together to prevent sabotage, are perfect targets for the attacking Japanese planes.

Only a handful of American fighters will rise to meet the enemy aircraft that Sunday morning.

19

SOUND BATTLE STATIONS!

WHAT'S HAPPENING?!

WE'RE UNDER ATTACK BY THE JAPANESE! MAN THE GUNS!

At the end of Battleship Row, the *Nevada* is struck by a single torpedo. It quickly begins firing back at the attacking planes.

Fuel oil spreads rapidly from where the torpedo has hit.

The *Nevada* is the only battleship to get underway that morning, but as it makes for the open sea, it is attacked by dive-bombers and begins to flood.

Lt. Commander Francis J. Thomas orders it to be beached rather than allowing it to sink and block the narrow harbor entrance.

Battleship Row is under furious attack by horizontal bombers, dive-bombers and fighters.

Even as the bombs fall, the ships return fire, surprising the Japanese attackers with the quick response of antiaircraft gunners from ships and shore batteries.

Fuel oil gushes from the torpedoed *Oklahoma* and *West Virginia*.

But time runs out for the battleship *Arizona*.

High-altitude bombers are dropping converted battleship shells, each weighing 1,760 pounds.

The fourth bomb to strike that day lands near the *Arizona*'s number two turret.

The *Arizona* is engulfed in a massive explosion caused by the bomb detonating the ship's own ammunition.

All 1,177 sailors and marines aboard it die almost instantly, including Captain Franklin Van Valkenburg and Fleet Commander Rear Admiral Isaac C. Kidd.

For the *Arizona*, the war is over. For the rest of America, it has just begun.

TORPEDO PLANES

Detroit

Raleigh

DIVE-BOMBERS

UTAH

Tangier

NEVADA

ARIZONA
Vestal

FORD ISLAND

TENNESSEE
WEST VIRGINIA

MARYLAND
OKLAHOMA

Neosho

CALIFORNIA

TORPEDO PLANES

HORIZONTAL BOMBERS

Shaw   PENNSYLVANIA

Cassin   Downes

PEARL HARBOR AND BATTLESHIP ROW

No battleship escapes the attack. The *Oklahoma* and the *Utah* are both capsized.

The *West Virginia* manages to counterflood to avoid the same fate. Fuel oil ignites and threatens to burn the ships as well as the men in the water.

23

There are many American heroes that Sunday morning.

Phillip Rasmussen is one of the few pilots to get his plane in the air. He is still wearing his pajamas when he engages the Japanese planes.

Aboard the *West Virginia*, Doris "Dorie" Miller mans a machine gun when its crew is killed. He will later receive the Navy Cross for bravery.

Fortunately for America, its own aircraft carriers are out to sea on exercises.

These carriers will form the backbone of the U.S. Navy in the coming years of war.

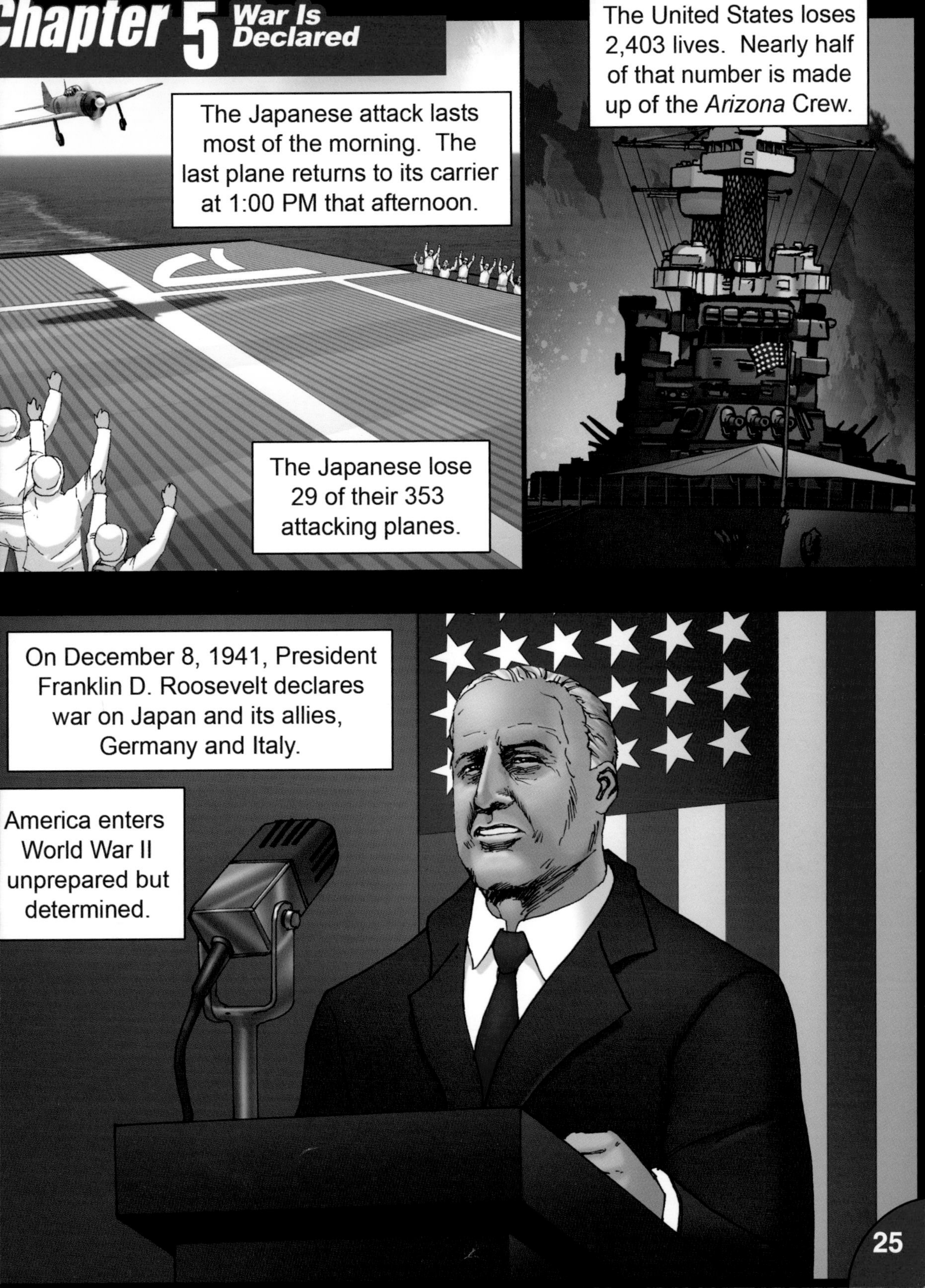

Chapter 5 War Is Declared
The Japanese attack lasts most of the morning. The last plane returns to its carrier at 1:00 PM that afternoon.
The Japanese lose 29 of their 353 attacking planes.
The United States loses 2,403 lives. Nearly half of that number is made up of the *Arizona* Crew.
On December 8, 1941, President Franklin D. Roosevelt declares war on Japan and its allies, Germany and Italy.
America enters World War II unprepared but determined.

The next four years are dark and terrible. America wages a war on two vast, deadly fronts, fighting across the Atlantic in Europe and in the endless Pacific Ocean.

America builds a war machine that will never be rivaled and brings her incredible resources of men and material to battle.

They fight in the air, on the ocean, under water, and on the islands, reaching ever closer to mainland Japan.

The American firestorm that finally reaches Japan is devastating.

The Japanese city of Hiroshima is struck by a single bomb. An atomic bomb.

Three days later, a second atomic bomb falls on the Japanese city of Nagasaki. The death toll is staggering.

On August 6, 1945, a single American B-29 bomber called the *Enola Gay* delivers a weapon the world has never seen before.

It is the end of Imperial Japan and World War II.

Tokyo Bay, Japan, September 2, 1945.

The battleship *Missouri* waits for the Japanese delegation to arrive to sign the official documents of surrender.

The signing table is near turret number two, the same place where, four years earlier, a Japanese bomb penetrated and destroyed the *Arizona*.

Today, the *Arizona* rests where it sank that day at Pearl Harbor.

A memorial has been built across the hull, and visitors from all over the world come to see it every year.

Drops of the *Arizona*'s fuel oil still rise to the surface of Pearl Harbor even after 65 years.

Today, the Battleship *Missouri* stands guard over Battleship Row, the *Arizona*, and all the Americans who died that Sunday morning.

The attack on Pearl Harbor will always be remembered, as will all the men and women who sacrificed their lives for their country.

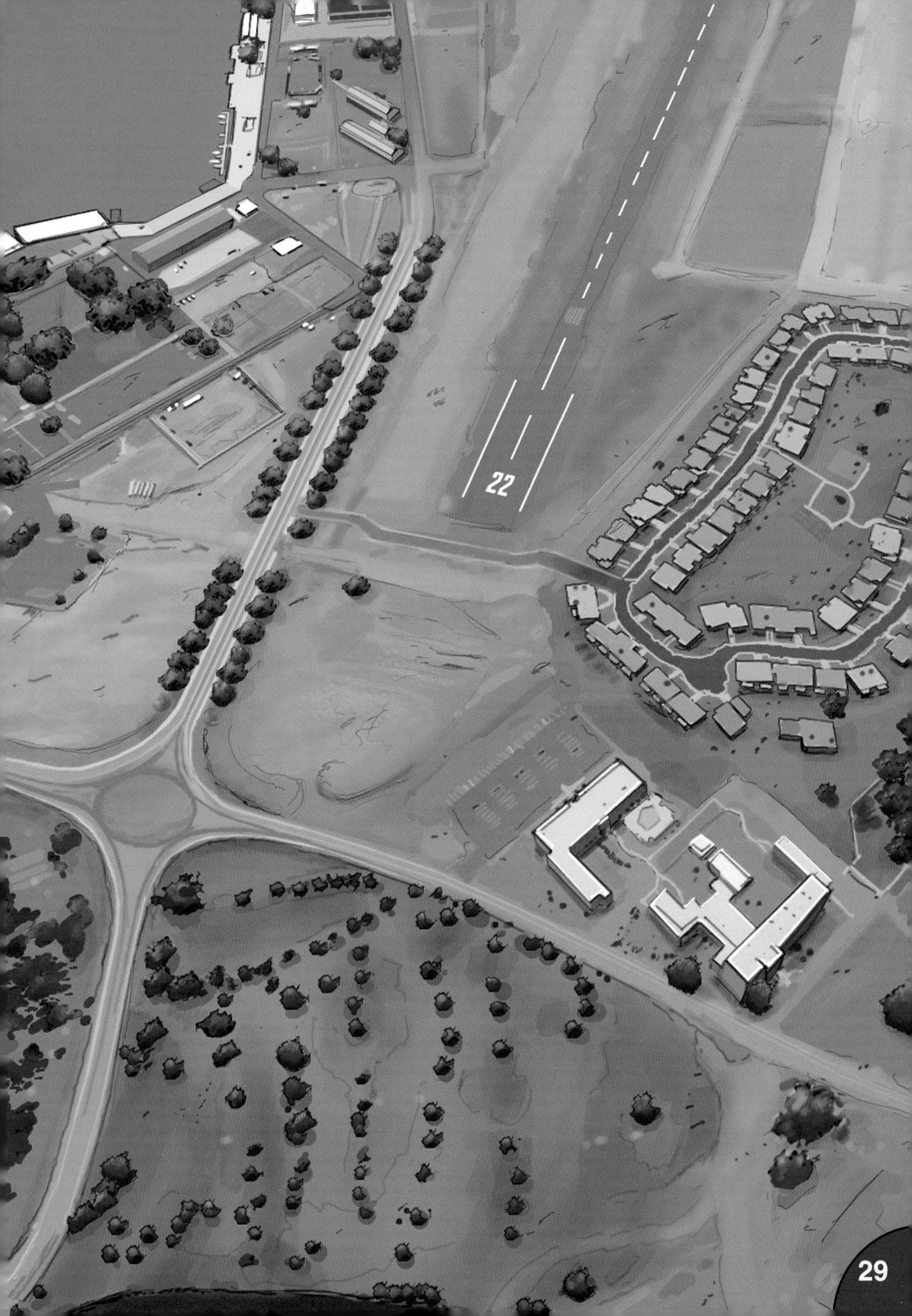
22

Timeline

1937 - Japan invaded North China.

1940 - The United States imposed a trade embargo to stop Japanese aggression.

1941 - In November, the Japanese sent a special envoy to the United States to discuss a diplomatic solution to Japanese expansion.

November 16, 1941 - The first submarines left Japan and sailed toward Pearl Harbor.

November 26, 1941 - The main Japanese fleet sailed for Pearl Harbor.

December 7, 1945 - The first wave of Japanese bombers and fighters began their attack on the air bases of Hawaii and then the Pacific Fleet. The attack continued for two and a half hours.

December 8, 1941 - President Roosevelt declared war on Japan and the Axis powers.

August 6, 1945 - The first atomic bomb was dropped on Hiroshima.

September 2, 1945 - The United States accepted the unconditional surrender from Japan on the battleship *Missouri*.

Glossary

aggressive - displaying strong or intense behavior that is often hostile.

capsize - to turn over.

detonate - to set off or explode.

Fascist - a member of a political philosophy that favors a dictatorship and places nation or race above individual rights.

Nazi - a member of the German political party that controlled Germany under Adolf Hitler.

reconnaissance - an inspection the military uses to gain information about enemy territory.

shogun - a military governor who ruled Japan. There was a line of shoguns until the revolution of 1867.

strafe - to fire at ground troops at close range. Strafing is usually done with machine-gun fire from an aircraft flying low to the ground.

Web Sites

To learn more about Pearl Harbor, visit ABDO Publishing Company on the World Wide Web at **www.abdopublishing.com.** Web sites about Pearl Harbor are featured on our Book Links page. These links are routinely monitored and updated to provide the most current information available.

Index

A
Akagi 4, 8, 10
American aircraft carriers 24
American airplanes 18, 19, 24, 26
Arizona, Battleship 21, 22, 25, 27, 28
atomic bomb 26

B
Battleship Row 17, 20, 21, 23, 28

C
California, Battleship 17
China 7
Chuichi Nagumo 4, 5

E
Enola Gay 26

G
Germany 7, 25

H
Hiroshima 26

I
Isoroku Yamamoto 5
Italy 7, 25

J
Japanese fleet 8, 9, 11, 13, 16, 17, 18, 19, 21, 25

K
Kidd, Isaac C. 22

M
Miller, Doris "Dorie" 24

Missouri, Battleship 27, 28
Mitsuo Fuchida 14

N
Nagasaki 26
Nevada, Battleship 17, 20

O
Oahu 12
Oklahoma, Battleship 17, 21, 23

P
Pearl Harbor Memorial 27, 28

R
Rasmussen, Phillip 24
Roosevelt, Franklin D. 25

S
Shigeru Itaya 10
shogun 6

T
Thomas, Francis J. 20
Tora Tora Tora 14
torpedoes 17, 20

U
Utah, Battleship 17, 23

V
Valkenburg, Franklin Van 22

W
West Virginia, Battleship 17, 21, 23, 24